Break Up.

Break Down.

Break Through.

GODSFORGE

Publisher – Godsforge. www.godsforge.com
Copyright © Geoff Olds

Title: Break Up. Break Down. Break Through.
Author: Olds, Geoff (1978—)
ISBNs: 978-0-6483679-6-3 (paperback)
            978-0-6483679-1-8 (epub)
            978-0-6483679-2-5 (mobi)
Subjects: Poetry

Images by Leanne Larson
Cover by Leanne Larson
Cover file creation by: Luke Harris at workingtype.com.au
Photo of author (page v) copyright © Tony Jong.

Dedicated to the Beautiful Spirit.

About the Author...

Geoff Olds has been an avid writer and poet since early teenage years. Over the past 15 years, he has focused his energy on building technology businesses, speaking at events and working as a volunteer counsellor.

Break Up. Break Down. Break Through. is a personal collection of poetry and writings on love – each entirely raw and honest. It is Geoff's first published work, soon to be followed by his novel *Death of an Entrepreneur*.

Geoff spends his spare time practicing martial arts, writing, travelling and helping others, which he believes is the greatest way a person can live a meaningful life.

You can read more at **www.geoffolds.com**

Break Up.
Break Down.
Break Through.

Geoff Olds

Published by
Godsforge

Author's Note

Love. What joy. What pain! This is a collection of writings, musings, agonies, poetry and experiences written with great rawness, pain, fear, care and vulnerability.

The key word is vulnerability. Something hard for a lot of men. Something even harder for business leaders, alpha types and those of us who instinctively look for other ways to numb the pain and block out feelings.

One of the key reasons I decided to publish this collection was because of the counselling I do for other men and because of the amazing advice from *The Way of a Superior Man* by David Deida.

In short, I counsel other men to be VULNERABLE with their feelings, their emotions, their partners and be willing to risk showing their underbelly. I hope they have learned from my repeated failings.

This book of rawness and vulnerability is my willingness (and yes, I am shaking when I type these words; fear is gripping me at thought of others reading this) to practice what I preach.

Is this collection a work of art? Is it worth reading?

And is it worth being published among the millions of other better works out there?

Intellectually I would say no. But spiritually I say hell yes!

Not because of the quality of the words; but the depth of emotion and pain that has gone into this.

I want to share this journey with everyone to show that I am a failure and a fuck up but there is a way through it all. So ultimately you can be the best version of yourself. I want others to understand that you can be abandoned and feel like your life is ending and you want to end it. BUT in the bitterness, brokenness and burned out smoking ruins of your life; the magical phoenix rises above.

I am indebted to my beautiful cousin Leanne Larson who transferred my scribbles and concepts into beautiful illustrations. I would also say a great heartfelt thanks to my editor Rachel Sadler who has polished this very rough piece of work. Jen Mosher was also very instrumental to helping us navigate through this maze of publishing. Thank you ever so much.

And finally, to those of you who have experienced even one percent of any of this: know that you are not alone, and you have my love, Agape, because there is a higher love.

Always and ever.

Geoff.

April 2018

Tragedies and the tearful voice of the troubadour,
Reminds us we are not alone,
Reminds us that we are all fools for love.

It's better to spill the blood of a quill;
than to spill the blood of our veins.

The Episodes

Break Up

The Heart was made to be Broken...
Oscar Wilde.

Shock.

What just happened?
Days ago, we were together,
Nothing could destroy us,
Was I that bad?

I used to sit in the park and wonder.
Now I just walk around and wander.
Lost my voice, I've become dumb.
This shock has made me completely numb.

No Contact.

From talking and thinking,
About someone every hour of the day.

To no contact.

This is worse than a prison sentence.

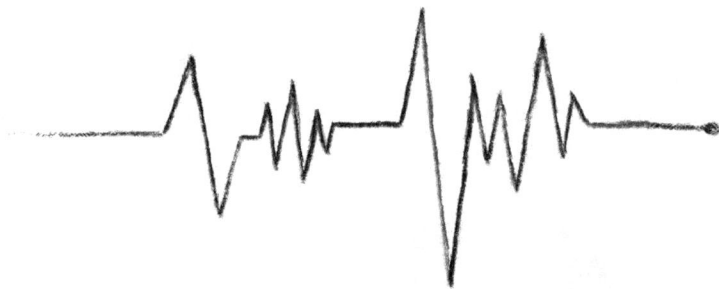

Long Story, Short Ending.

It was meant to start at a wedding,
But this long story has a short ending.
Like a single dot brings a finish,
The end came in a single minute.

If you added up thousands of hours,
You'd have war and peace and faulty towers.
An epic saga with drama strange,
Shakespearean plots with shades of grey.

Love is a complex consuming beast,
Ending abruptly with laying of wreath.
Countless hours of highs and lows,
Punctured by reality and awful throes.

Why did God weave love with pain?
Why did he give us tears like rain?
When was it cool to distort fairy-tale?
Why do miracles dissolve and fail?

This strong crazy consuming emotion,
Takes a heart to burn in devotion.
Why when we are so attached,
Do we ruin our chances with perfect match?

It was a long story with short ending,
A bitter pill to kick-start mending.
This story was meant to be for life,
But life ends with whimpering bells of strife.

And I, this poet has played the fool,
I've failed again and broken the rule.
As tales are told and transcribed in hell,
This author has inked page with bloody quill.

Left to recount memories in purgatory,
A sorry sad mess with no ending glory.
Bitterness of deadly wicked sins,
The bleakness of no goal to win.

A single false seed is all it takes,
To bury the mind and painfully raze.
If you are smart loyal and true,
Don't join me here in heartbreak blues.

Truth and the Original Sin.

You broke up with me...

But I broke you first.

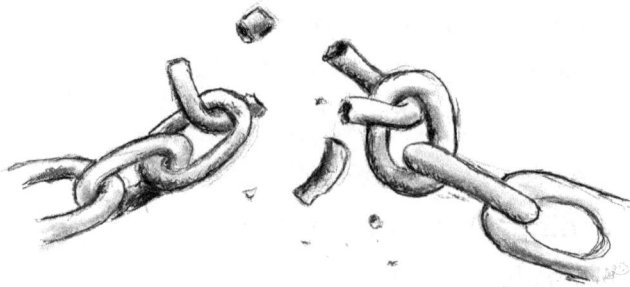

Save Me.

Save me from this heartbreak,

Save me from this pain.

Won't anyone save me?

(But **only** if you know her name.)

Doing Time.

Cast out of heaven
The gates slammed shut
Fallen from grace
Desperate to see her face

No answers to my messages
No responses to entreaties
Just white space and noise
And time's razor claws

Wandering alone
No fire to burn
No way to turn
Just a heart to yearn.

The crime was committed
Justice served
The only thing left is mercy
And love's divine sympathy.

Just serving time
Every minute a stab
Walking on broken glass
Nothing but painful past.

Just doing time.
Painfully, slowly, lonely.
Solitary confinement.
Lack of alignment.

Natural Justice.

Condemned in minutes.
Punished forever.

Agony of Rejection.

There's no pain like love's rejection,
The coldness of a snapped connection.
The darkness of a shattered soul,
The blackness of the deepest hole.

You scream in loud and audible pain,
You rail against the lashing rain.
Life takes colour and replaces with grey
Once you had love and now it's razed.

Four walls of a broken apartment,
Ceiling pitched with evil hatred.
Floors like the blades of hell,
Windows showing the shadows in veil.

You reach out in madness with boiling sorrow,
The days end in failure, without tomorrow.
Hope is lost in shattered reality,
Colourful town turned evil city.

Just one word, one response, you cry,
The silence is returned in terms so vile.
The emptiness sinks in with devilish delight,
Day gives way to torturous night.

Whatever the way, the reason or why,
Your only answer is a muted sigh.
Energy goes to an unearthed pit
The lure of sleep never quits.

Love makes fool of many man,
Life hangs by like tattered plan.
Loneliness hangs on trumped up flag,
Every night leaves only a stinking rag.

The demons of the past shout and writhe,
The bitterness of failure makes forfeited life.
No comfort is accepted, given or received,
The heart is broken and fatefully deceived.

In the end, shadows begin to conspire,
The mind is tricked with awful fire.
Vitality is driven with bloody dejection,
Can any man survive this awful rejection?

Music.

Why is music twice as loud
When falling in love?

And deafening when
Cast out of love?

Doubt.

You doubted me...

But you will never doubt me,
Like I doubt myself.

Blocked.

Thank God she blocked me.

In my darkest hour,
I lost my willpower.

Ashamed, a fool,
I broke the rule.

And as a desperate man,
Without any plan.

I hit send,
Trying to make amends.

Now I know I erred,
'Cause I send her bleeding words.

Thank God she blocked me.

Dante Walked Past.

Dante walked past.
Not fast. Slow.
Each step was excruciating.
Painstaking.
Grating.
Hands shaking.
Heart breaking.

She was there.
Beautiful. Elegant.
Each breath heavenly inspiration.
Above her station.
Queen of nation.
Beautiful incarnation.
Source of salvation.

Dante's heart pounded.
Skin tingled. Pulse quickened.
Woman of desire.
Hearts raging fire.
Longing sigh.
Secret ire.
Death on a pyre.

She was alive.
But she was gone.
He was alone.
Life's empty throne.
Mind's constant drone.
Water to foam.
No place for home.

Dante's memory.
Haunted him constantly.
Of hopefully dances.
Of lost romances.
Sidelong glances.
Love's trances.
Lost chances.

As he walked past.
He couldn't help but look.
Eyes met together.
Souls connected.
Choices regretted.
Hearts neglected.
Destinies rejected.

Beatrice's eyes held fast.
And Dante walked past.

One Kiss.

In the mist we kissed.
But miss,
I didn't know,
That kiss would mean,
I would miss,
Miss you,
So much more.

Did You Just…?

I hope I am wrong.
I sincerely hope I am.

I've spent all my life,
Looking for someone,
Who'd let me give up on myself,
And give in to them.

But did you just give in to yourself,
And give up on me?

Lonely Stranger.

He sits there
Head in hands
Slumped
Dumped
Heart broken
Nothing's spoken

The repeated tunes
Play endlessly
Soulful
Woeful
Heart's cold
Day's getting old

The tree casts shadows
A perfect metaphor
Gloom
Doom
Head's hurting
Eyes burning

He stares at a phone
It's bitterly cold
Silent
Mind's violent
No response
Muscles tense

There's no energy
Hearts cast apart
Shattered
Nothing matters
Crying on the inside
Losing the fight

The pain's immense
Girl gone, gone girl
Defeat
Empty seat
He's bleeding
Shallow breathing

I know his pain
Been there, was there
Lonely
Empty
Wearing a mask
Fading fast

Right and Left.

You were Right.

So I was Left.

Apartment: Meant to be Apart.

I'm standing alone on this balcony,
In this apartment,
And I know we were meant to be apart.

It's a sad scene,
Staring out in the night,
Solitary figures sit on their balconies.

There are so many of us,
So many; but still alone,
Hermits hanging out in hell.

Even the slightest acknowledgement,
Sends a sad, sad signal,
To another broken heart across the street.

Apartment,
Meant to be apart.
On broken hearts boulevard.

We should all be booked in,
To heartbreak hotel.
Sipping on gin and tonics,

But the only tonic,
For broken souls,
Is the solace of The One?

Foolishly we turn to old love songs,
Trying to find righted wrongs,
But words only tear us apart.

Apartment,
Meant to be apart.
On broken hearts boulevard.

Angry phone calls,
Bitter words thrown around.
Sad contemplation lasts.

Unanswered emails,
Wayward females,
Men gone to lovers' homes.

A block of solitary cells,
The only calls are ones that sell,
And lights sadly twinkling.

Apartment,
Meant to be apart.
On broken hearts boulevard.

Empaths.

Empaths feel heartbreak twice.

Alone on New Year's Eve.

All I have done wrong,
Has led me to this point.
A cracked spirit, a broken soul,
Alone on New Year's Eve.

Happy couples stroll past,
Dreams intact, love growing.
But for some of us;
It's just a fracturing fairy-tale.

There's music everywhere.
Lights flashing, souls dancing,
Families smile in the lamplight,
While dreaming of the next journey.

And the deck pounds with footsteps,
People going places,
Going to destinations,
Going somewhere, anywhere.

But I'm trapped here.
Dressed up with no gate to walk through,
Just left with Killers singing.
And the bitterness of failure.

Sometimes dreams don't come true.
We're stuck with what might have been,
Stuck rooted with this shadow,
And the mind's constant barrage.

Somehow, we plucked the feathers,
And fashioned a million darts,
That we hurl at our hearts,
Tainted with the mind's deep poison.

A solitary lap, and another again.
Sucking on poisonous air,
Randomly being hit with revelry.
But this weary soul can't face it.

The fire has gone out,
Though fire spurts and sparks fly.
This dry withered soul is empty.
Fuel has no effect.

One step in the wrong direction,
A journey into purgatory,
A damning sentence,
66 years making love to regret.

One shot, it's just one shot.
One shot at redemption.
Why can't I see the exit
From this wearing wilderness?

Alone on New Year's Eve,
Surrounded by lovers,
Crowds everywhere,
One man, one state, one fate.

Sage Words.

I was told I'd meet an angel like you.
A wise man once said to me.
You will find the one.
The one who you'll give everything up for.

The wise man was right.

He just didn't tell me,
That she wouldn't stick around.

Wait, What?

Wait... what?

How can you switch off love so quickly?

Still Alive (Somewhere).

Still alive, that may be the evil.
I'm fading and wading through treacle.
But somewhere, anywhere,
There's hope and I'm aware.

When you ghosted me,
I thought you were leaving to be free.
But as far as I can look and see,
Neither of us are free, just at sea.

I want that sweet release,
The release that is death and peace.
Ironically, I want to give up the ghost,
But somehow, you're alive in this host.

It's not even seven degrees apart,
You seem right there, in my heart.
It's agony and pain in double,
How long can I stay out of this trouble?

There's a two-edged sword striking me.
The life inside comes with the fee.
The price is a high and terrible tax.
Any moment I'll kneel to the axe.

Only I hope that when it falls,
It really falls and there's no more.
But somehow, I think this beautiful spirit,
Just simply won't dissipate.

Forgive Me.

Forgive me.
Not because you want to.
Not because you need to.

But because there are no stones
To be thrown.

I'm flawed, I've failed.

Am I Satan to be cast out of this Heaven?
To wander forever in this Hell?

Turns out I'm no angel,
But nor am I a demon.

The truth is I'm a human on the up.
And so are you.

So, forgive me for my failings.
Even in this blind state,
I know it's not the right fate,
And you also need forgiveness.

Because you are perfectly imperfect.

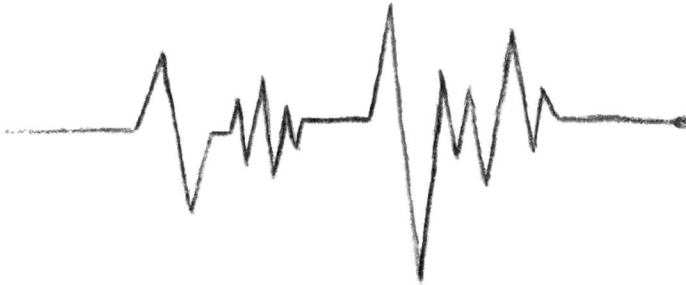

Sunglasses.

Forgive me,
For wearing these sunglasses.
Inside.

Because if I don't,
You would see me,
Inside.

What Do You Do?

What do you do
When your tears
Are stuck;

Somewhere between
The hollowness of
Your stomach
And the pain in your chest?

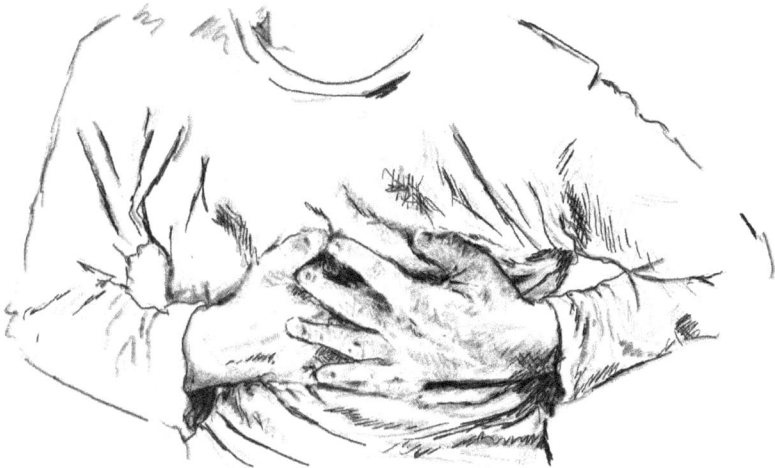

The Mask.

Another day, another task,
Another routine, don the mask.
Pull on the suit, buckle the belt,
Block her out, forget how you felt.

Just because you're numb,
Doesn't mean you're dumb.
Take the pill, keep the nausea down,
Paint on the smile, don't frown.

Delete the memories, don't ask why,
If you break down, step outside to cry.
Leave the office, let go of sad,
Get into the gym, go mad.

Don't try to change or escape,
Take the pain and don your cape.
You are going to want to collapse,
But your duties to others can't lapse.

Feed your sorrow on the sad songs,
Beat yourself up with all your wrongs.
Fill your heart with all the grief,
Don't let others in like an oiled thief.

This is you, you and you alone,
This whole space is yours to own.
There are no more questions to ask,
Just rise up quickly and choose a mask.

Give up the Ghost.

I understand Jesus better.
When it said,
He gave up the Ghost.

He did it. Willingly.

Love Hard, Leave Harder.

Here I am. Breaking, shattering.
Just when I hit rock bottom,
A part of my soul cracks further.
Can the crumbs of my heart dissipate?
Can they break further so there's nothing else?
So that what I once had becomes invisible?

Perhaps that's how you want it.
To grind me up so there's nothing left?
You threatened me once;
More than once, you told me you love hard,
But you leave hard and you hit hard!

You think silence is not violence?
Does rejection not feed fresh dejection?
Not a word, not a motion,
Nothing to meet my daily devotion.
Except the crushing of second hand abuse,
And I can say from it; there is no refuge.
I can't even say I'm a shadow anymore.

Perhaps I'm just a shadow of a shadow.
Maybe a chalk outline of the man struck down,
Or perhaps the final drop from the bloody crown.
Either way take the number zero and divide it 77 ways,
That's how I am since you've been gone, 77 days.

You left an imperfect man, a work in progress.
Your accusations still rob him of sleep.
If only I could take my fright and make it fight,
Or even flight or something other than panic.
I wounded you, but you don't know my love,
You were and are the great pearl of price.
With joy I gave it all up, up for you.

The unicorn, the sweet ray of sunlight.
And now I'm wandering around decaying wood,
Where no sunshine lights up at all.
And the search for that musical, mystical creature,
Is long gone; just the scars of its wounds and trampling.

Am I not worthy of your love? Are you chasing perfect?
Don't you know perfect means thorough work?
Am I to be crucified for hours or minutes of failure?
For ill speech, for my stumbling, for hard words?
Am I to be condemned forever?
Where's the forgiveness; the beautiful spirit?

Oh, how too bitter the thought is,
Of you turning to others in this hell.
All I can do is take the stabbing pains to my chest.
But I want to hold you, kneel in front of you.
To ask for forgiveness, to ask that you remember,
Not 1pc, not a few hours, but a lifetime.

One day I will die. I pray for my death soon.
Because this cord of love is bursting from my soul.
Each moment I fall weaker, I have no voice.
You'd rather listen to that voice in your head.
Your trusted advisor's call and there's plenty of fish.
So, I pray for my death. Take this away God. Take it away.

Jesus knelt with blood on his brow.
He took the whip on his back to blood.
For me I kneel, vomiting because of this grief,
And the pain I take, I take willingly.
Oh, that you avenge your anger and injustice,
On my body instead of stabbing my soul.

My friends think I'm a fool, they look with pity.
And the three wise women, throw bile.
Others judge me, thinking I'm in the vicious cycle.
Oh Lord if they even felt a heartbeat or a fragment of my soul,
I would ask that they leave me, abandon me.

So, you love hard. You leave hard.
You hit hard. If only you left me scarred.
Instead I'm free falling, after failing.
And while I'm dying your ship's sailing.
I can see clearly now beautiful spirit,
Though you slay me, I'll keep falling for you.

Weep.

Sometimes I weep,
For the love lost.

But mostly I weep,
For the darkness,
That has replaced it.

Break Down

Even those who never frown,
eventually break down.
Linkin Park.

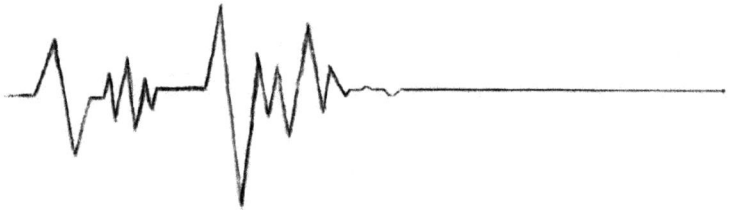

Destruction.

If I'm going to face destruction,

I will make it self-destruction.

That way the end,
Will be my end.

Thank You, Dear Friends.

Thank you, dear friends.
Thank you for your judgement.
Thank you for kicking this pitiful dog.

Thank you for the extra scars.
Thank you for the additional reminders.
Thank you for your hardness.

Thank you for your tough love.
Thank you for your berating.
Thank you for casting me as the villain.

You have taught me well.
You have taught me to forgive.
When my heart was as cold as tomb.
When all I could grasp was real doom.

Salt into the wounds,
A blindfold in the gloom.
Thank you, dear friends,
I'll always forgive until the end.

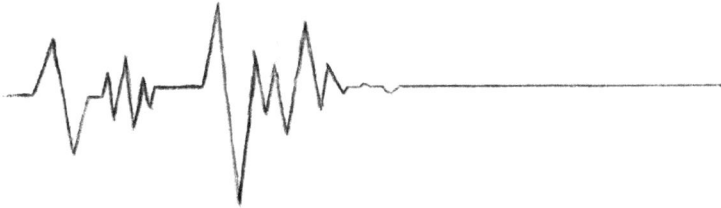

The Man I Hate.

I used to be the prince of the day,
All my steps went in the right way.
A gallant chivalrous people's man,
I launched forward with life's plan.

I saw great beauty and blue skies,
I'd be ready to give my life and die.
Yes, I was once a kingly soul,
A courageous man without hole.

But now I'm a man I hate,
Broken, bitter, consumed by fate.
Lying alone in stinking gutter,
Tone deaf and with shaking stutter.

The mirror screams back Sinner!
Brown eyes accuse and cinder.
Failed life and torn purpose,
Ruined journey, shameful surface.

Though I tear at my flesh like a madman,
I can't stop the feeling of being damned.
I'm broken and in a dire strait,
I've become the man I hate.

But one redemption remains,
If I can wash my soul and remove the stain,
If I can bath myself in pure flood,
Maybe I can be the man I love.

Dead on the Inside.

I joined a club today.
A beautiful woman welcomed me.
She smiled with everything but her eyes.

And told me sweetly;
"Welcome to the Dead on the Inside Club."
I asked her how long she'd been a member.
She said to me,
Chillingly and willingly,
Without resignation or hesitation;
"Eight hundred and forty-eight days."

And I knew why,
We all know the exact day.
That day zero,
That our sentence begins.

Fading to Black.

At times my ego's been a white horse,
A proud stallion.
I've been as proud as punch,
Like a heavyweight boxer.

I've often felt I can do anything.
Like some sort of demigod.
I've crafted a future like no other;
An incredible inventor.

Yes, I have strode the world,
In my mind a titan.
I've more ideas about life,
Than the philosophers of old.

But now I feel my frailty,
Like a dying man on a field.
I feel like I have nothing to offer;
Just a beggar.

Life has proven me wrong,
Many times.
Yes, many times I've been a fool,
A very foolish man.

I've chased false quests,
To please myself.
I've laughed like a madman,
Like a babbling brook.

Now I'm just a shell,
A shell of a former person.
This knight has failed,
Misery has set in.

This malaise doesn't seem to go,
Like an eternal fog.
Sleep is filled with nightmares,
Nightmares filled with regrets.

Lying here I can see,
Sleep is my solace.
Yes, I'm fading to black,
Just fading to black.

Pain in the Past.

When is the past just the past?
Life seems rushing too fast.
All this pain and sorrow
Does it catch me tomorrow?

Am I ruined, am I broken?
Has the rain stopped soaking?
Vaporous signals of the fallen
Constant evidence of the rotten.

The enemy lies in shadows
Reminders of prior failures.
Am I a hollow collection of parts?
The old wound pains and smarts.

Is there a narrative of redemption?
Some logical storied correction.
Something to hold and follow
A depth out past the shallows.

If only I could let go
From the disasters that show.
If only I could catch on to life
Rest and peace from this strife.

To Think of You.

To think of you hurting like this,
Kills me.

To think of you with utter sadness,
Destroys me.

To think of your hatred for me,
Makes me bleed.

To think of you despising me,
Makes me despise myself.

To think of those voices in your ear,
Makes me violently ill.

To think of you alone,
Makes me so lonely.

To think of you weeping,
Hurts me so much.
To think of you in pain,
Makes me fall.

To think of you.
Makes me blame myself.
Makes me hate myself.
Makes me loathe myself.

I'm to blame.
And salvation's lost.

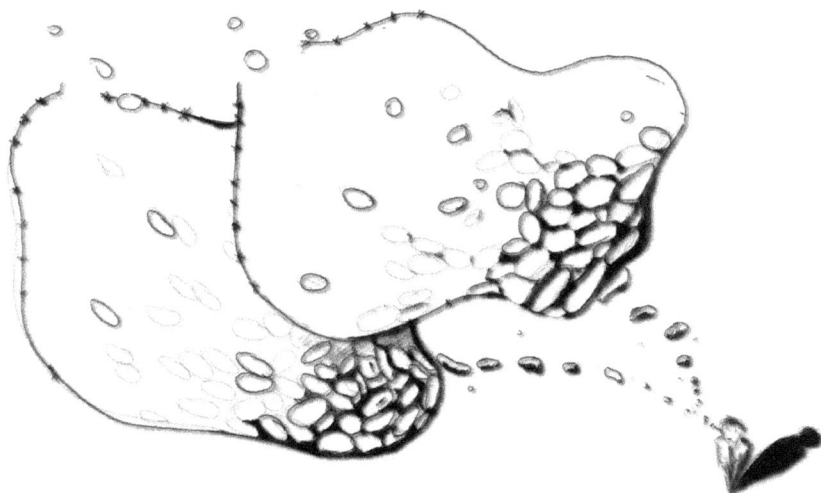

Memories.

I'm sitting here in this empty place
With a spectre with invisible face
There's no comfort in my companion
As she's gone with no retraction.

Yeah, I'm all by myself
All by myself in no such wealth
I may have money and things
But this place just hollow rings.

And with me is memories
Of bittersweet past
That went so fast
Just memories and myself.

I have one fatal terrible flaw
A blot on my soul and a cruel claw
I'm lost in the pursuit of the perfect
It is an awful ruining defect.

I didn't recognise the green grass
I left it to get dry and lifeless
My mind was lost in forward fantasy
Chasing some impossible ecstasy.

And now I'm lost in memory
Memories so faint but real
Memories that grab and feel
Pictures of the past and memories.

It's hard to know where it all went wrong
But I know that I should; I wasn't strong
I didn't fight for what was right
I walked out cold and numb into the night.

I could have been with her
I could have been consumed by her allure
But instead the songs don't lighten
They chime away and frighten.

Yes, these memories are painful
Projections in my mind
And I'm losing what's mine
These memories are fateful.

Memories.
Memories calling.
Memories.
I'm falling.
Memories. Memories.

One of Those Days.

If I could speak to you.
You may bless me.
With a little ordinary conversation.
Like how was your day?
With that voice of an angel.
And I would just say;
My day was absolutely *&^^%%#(*%]
And there was a small respite...
And then it was $*&%(#&%)#)*$
You would politely cough and wish me well.
Not knowing the day was perfectly fine,

But without you it was simply (#&$^$ing hell.

Do You Know What It Is like...?

Do you know what it is like?
To know your closest,
Your nearest,
Your dearest,
Your sweetest,
Would rather smile and talk to a stranger?

Than the man who used to be;
Your closest,
Your nearest,
Your dearest,
Your sweetest.

Or was I simply delusional?

Illness.

By now I should have been cured...

Perhaps this is terminal?

Here Lies a Man.

Here lies a man,
He appears alive,
But is very much dead.

Now where do the undead rest?

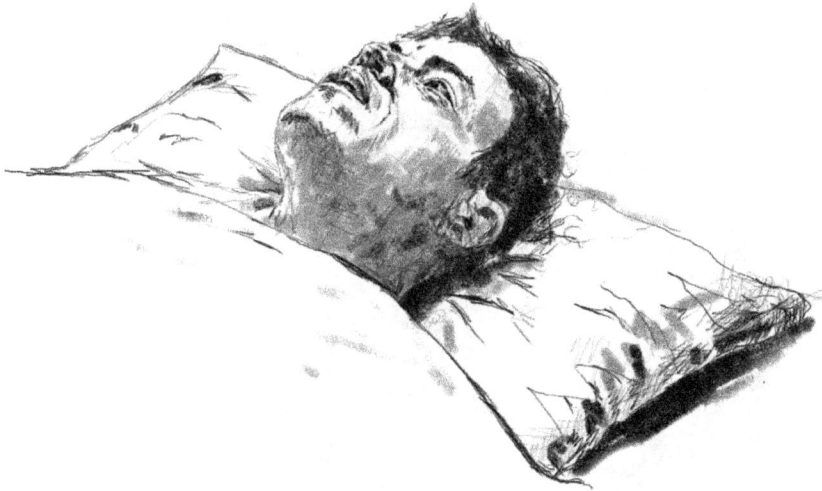

Behind the Mask.

I saw you. You saw me.
I heard your words.
I reacted to your words.
You reacted to my words.

You saw my actions.
You heard my words.
You acted. I acted.

If only I had seen and heard your thoughts and feelings.
I would have acted differently.

Closure.

A fatal wound remains,
I should be dead by now,
But this vacant hollow shell,
Carries on, lives on.

I can taste the executioner's sweat,
The cold steel rests on my neck,
I wait for the final blow,
But time goes on, lasting forever.

The verdict has been passed,
The final letter lays on my chest,
Though it is over something lives,
Something lives on, something remains.

I know that I can take the blame,
I know it's game over
But I still don't understand,
And this confused life lives on.

My mind longs for one final encounter,
Not for mercy or a stay of execution,
I long for the voice of closure,
But only silence comes along.

I desire a way to close the door,
So another can be opened,
So the phoenix can rise from the ashes,
But only this zombie wanders.

Dear Plato.

Love is not just a serious mental illness,
Dear Plato.

Love is more than losing your mind,
Dear Plato.

Love is a twisted joke,
From the maddest of the Gods.

Think on this;
Dear Plato.

Heart.

How many times can a heart be destroyed,
Before it is irreparable?

Soulless Solace.

Alone. Left to his own devices.
The pain cries out, for many vices.
The mind spins like a top,
Heart's grinding like a wrecker's shop.

This solace is soulless.
This situation is helpless.
It's penitent solitary confinement,
Life's bloody exhausting refinement.

Did the crime, do the time.
But there's no end to this miserable clime.
Time drags on in this self-imposed asylum,
The madness comes in desperate rhyme.

The man rages in muted claim,
He cuts himself in blinded flame,
He loathes life with acid tongue,
He rails with the world and what it's done.

The mirror spits flames in wild fury,
An image guilty by the harshest jury,
A prisoner by deed and awful action,
Life's ardent painful natural reaction.

There's no way through this impossible breakdown,
No clown can erase this permanent frown,
Skies are marred, clouds are brown,
Hell has opened up and spewed demons loud.

Hot feels cold, heat like ice,
Thoughts cascade down like horded lice.
The body itches, skin flakes away,
Negativity crashes like dirty ocean spray.

Find yourself, love yourself, they cry,
But deep inside there's only a groaning Why!
Only a dying man's audible sigh,
Wings ruptured off like a tortured fly.

There is no hope, no salvation,
It's the bleakest of times in this damned nation,
Kingdom has come, and Lord has ruled,
This prisoner chained, perpetually fooled.

Weighed Down.

My eyes are dull.
The sky is grey.
I'm faced with a haze,
In a daze.

Stunned,
I'm gunned down.
I'm so sorry for this frown,
No movement, I'm bound.

Corpse, just a corpse,
Sad to say, sad to report.
Fallen way too short,
Now I'm nearly naught.

Even on this evenin'
Far from feeling even.
Hands just shaking.
Heart still breaking.

Want to curl up.
Put me in a ball,
Let others have a ball,
Just leave, don't call.

I'll get there,
Just don't care,
Prefer this dark cave,
I'm the fog's willing slave.

Self-pity,
In this selfish city.
Pity about this self,
Lost wealth, losing health.

Grey skies,
Warm bed,
Paralytic legs,
Roll over, let go.

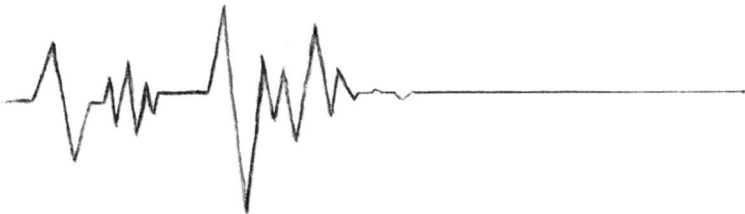

Song of the Universe.

I want you to hear the song of the universe,
Yes, every beautiful goddamn verse.

Because if you heard this verse,
You might go into reverse.

Damned.

This time it's a special kind of hell,
Not sure when or how I fell.
I sure as hell know the overall why,
Maybe the hell is in saying goodbye.

Right now, all I can do is burn,
All those emotions I can't unlearn.
I can't un-see that beautiful smile,
This burning, my God, turn down the dial.

But as usual there's no real answer,
Just all that pain of memories dancing.
The blackness of the unslept mind,
The cruelty, torturous and horribly unkind.

Even Dante had Beatrice to guide,
But when she comes into my mind,
All I can do is feel pain and cry,
And haunting, so haunting, memory of why.

At this point it feels like the end,

Nothing is right, nothing will mend.

Even your friends, have become fiends,

Their view is simply you're beyond amends.

They don't see you here; slowly roasting,

Slowly withering, no time for posting.

And when you show that underbelly,

In goes the knife; as easy as jelly.

Tough love is what is always sold,

But how many times do you have to be told?

Words are thrown like flaming darts,

Those fiery darts, hit straight to the heart.

All I can do is completely shut down,
Don the mask and play the clown.
Then secretly weep as the quietly damned,
Let out secret drops, previously dammed.

Do the crime, you do the time.
Sweat through this, feverish clime.
I'll emerge, some day; I'll find a way.
Just not now, not right now, not today.

On My Own.

The hours blend into days.
The days into weeks.
Now the weeks into months.

There's just the same feeling.
Repeating over and over.
It's Groundhog Day, but I'm no Bill Murray.

I'm stuck in this purgatory.
The time trap has been set.
The only clock is the mirror; I'm beginning to avoid.

Rinse and repeat is the order.
Except I'm only clean on the outside.
Haunted voices are always reminding me.

A raging debate occurs in my head;
You are wrong, you're a failure
Versus how you could let one person destroy you?

The only way to make the voices stop
Is duty and the responsibility to be there.
I'm very aware that I'm only just there.

The strength is coming in the loneliness.
No more cruel words from so called friends,
No more expectations of love or care.

No more desire, no more lust,
I do what I must, I do just enough.
Solitude is my salvation.

There is no more reason to be a hit.
There is just enough energy to quit.
I know it, I feel it, I'm on my own.

Everyone Goes Away.

Baby it's true, I'm a dangerous man,
Don't go there, don't become a fan.
I'm a wrecking ball in motion,
So, don't get any ideas on devotion.

Let me put it straight to you,
Let me give you a solid clue.
There's no point in an investment,
Because I trade in perpetual resentment.

(This is a sad traveller...)

Because everyone goes away
No one seems to want to stay
This is my fate
This my lonely state
I'm a walking hex
I'm a failing bet
Because everyone goes away.

I know it's completely me
People think I'm free
But I'm telling you now
It'll end, and I can tell you how.

You see at some point
I will only disappoint
I'll withdraw and be absent
And no one will know what is meant.

(This is a lonely traveller...)

Because everyone goes away
No one seems to want to stay
This is my fate
This my lonely state
I'm a walking hex
I'm a failing bet
Because everyone goes away.

The truth is I hardly understand myself
I've lost my happy inner health
I'm stumbling and confused
Just whistling the cold old blues.

The confidence has gone
The king has left the throne
Leaving a wake of people
The roof is broken, a collapsed steeple.

Because everyone goes away
No one seems to want to stay
This is my fate
This my lonely state
I'm a walking hex
I'm a failing bet
Because everyone goes away.

Yeah, I'm destined to go alone
I'm convicted and disowned
I'm a constant misfit
I'm stricken, lost, stripped.

(This is an eternal traveller...)

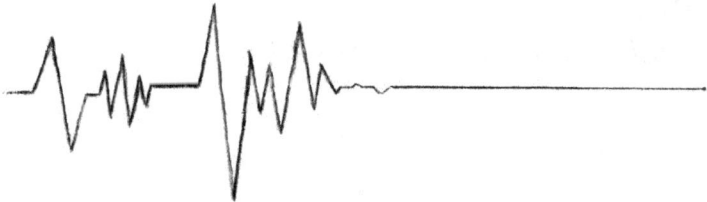

Amiel.

I want Amiel,
The woman who is Obsessed;
Where have you gone?

I want those beautiful words,
Each morning;
I Love You.

Vulnerable.

Like days of old,
We have our weak spots.

A small tiny spot,
But to strike there is death.

I know how Achilles felt.
When he followed his passions.
When he followed his purpose.
It took one flight of the dart,
To crush his will and all his heart.

Maybe some of us are not able,
To live a life so vulnerable?

Words That Do You Justice.

I have written words,

In the below box,

That actually do you justice.

Words that when cast into the box,

Pay true homage,

To that smile,

That amazing dark hair,

The intensity of your eyes,

How your hugs feel,

And what it is like,

To wake up next to you.

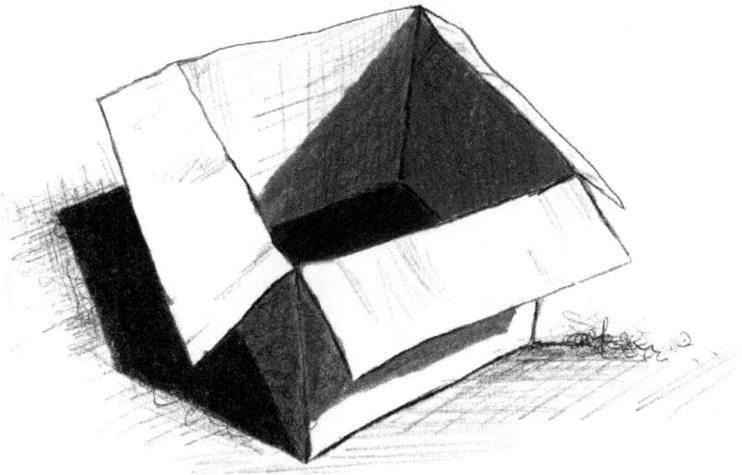

Attached.

I can't function.
I'm hardwired to this attachment.
The code is looking for the missing code.

I'm aware of this software.

Goddammit!

Fire the fucking programmer.

Liquid Destruction.

So subtle, your hold on me.
Violently and quietly you strip me
Of Dignity, Respectability and Capability.

You creep around, you're everywhere.
And when we lock lips, there is no care
For Tomorrow, Sorrow or Life so Hollow.

Blended, you fit into the environment.
You are so damn easy to swallow;
You are meant to be consumed, but you consume.

Under your powers we are loose and lost.
Wanting false dreams and fateful illusions;
Reality is Shattered, Battered and Mad Hatted.

Even with you, the wise become fools.
When they hold you and kiss you;
Intoxicated, Deflated, Berated, Ill Fated.

The best among us are children.
And caring parents warding you away;
There's no chance to fall under your sway.

You slowly strip away mankind.
Of its prudence and sound mind;
Depraved, Craved, Waved and Dismayed.

You're a terrible mistress,
You hunt to hand out distress.
Your victims are all and ready to fall.

But fuck you and your seduction!
I deny you and your addiction;
Without you there is only love and hope.

You've played your hand, you are done.
Your promise of fun has had its run.
Stay away and in your prison place.

Reality has its own perfect beauty.
Fresh air and fresh heads getting ahead;
Away from your poison and toxic nature.

Love Hangover.

Dammit, why is my head hurting all over?
Why am I struggling to breathe?
Why is my heart so crazy heavy?
Why can I only feel a desperate need?

Some days I can barely walk,
Some days nothing makes sense,
Some days the only thing is a pillow over the head,
And a prayer that one day I will mend.

I know I am only half functioning,
I guess that's a slight improvement,
From a man collapsed in a foreign city,
And a lost soul ready to be buried in cement.

But now I cry from all the pain,
And when it's grey, and it rains,
I scream with a sad delight inside,
Because it's the only weather that I can claim.

Oh, I walked away from simplicity and peace,
Because of hallucinating and all the masks,
The walls were crumbling and falling,
Only quicksand and paper-thin tasks.

Now it's twisted memories and soft roses,
That visit with a sweet scent,
But bring an immortal sadness,
With mixed feelings and lost sentiment.
Oh, I wish I could burn it all away,

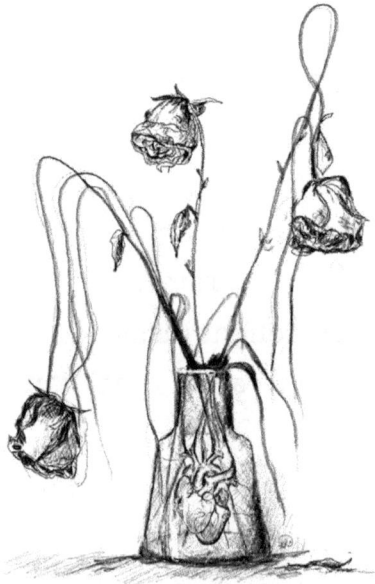

I wish this dull thudding would dissipate,
I wish the phoenix could rise again,
And take me away from my sorrowful fate.

Am I going to hell?
Am I in a self-afflicted purgatory?
Or am I beating myself into a martyred story?
Questions worthy of asking and answering.

Even the glasses I wear are scratched,
My vision impaired and rattled,
A tremor in the hand and in the mind,
A fragile pathway for the battered.

Maybe I just need time,
To reach up and climb out of this slime,
To heal completely,
And begin again.

Either way, I just have to keep going.
And whatever happens, I hope to see the sun shining.

If Only You Really Left.

It feels like just yesterday you left.
So sharp and quick and hard.
Like a banshee shriek.
Or a slap from an Amazon.
Like a wrinkle in time.
Like Thor's lightning.

But God! If only you had really left.

Because then I wouldn't taste you in Sushi.
Or feel you waiting just around the corner.
Or hear you singing Taylor Swift,
With the innocence of a new born child.

I most certainly wouldn't feel your pain,
I wouldn't be punishing myself,
I wouldn't be waiting for your email,
Or looking forward to our next travels.

Why didn't you leave,
When you left?

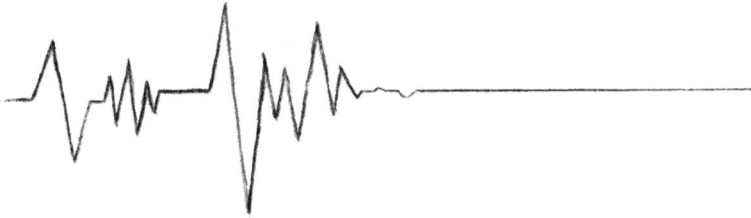

No Answers.

I wish I had the answers to all
To clearly make sense of why we fall.
I would proclaim it to the world
Clarify all that is blurred.

The mist and fog would disappear
The whole purpose would be clear
We could let go of all fears
Find the path we should steer.

There'd be no more wars
Enmity and hate, no longer roars
We'd smile and have love
Give destruction the shove.

Oh, I wish I had the answers
I long for responded prayers
I'd go on any mission
To find life's reason.

'S.

You left and whispered,
To yourself;
"Let Go."

If only you'd turned,
And said;
"Let's Go."

Decision.

People speak to me like I'm a robot.
Like I can just hit delete.
Like I can just swipe this away.
Like I have some mysterious power.

Some say I'm to blame,
I agree, to my shame,
But that doesn't stop me,
Quietly whispering her name.

Some say she's not the one,
They tell me to get back and have fun.
But behind the clouds,
I, of all people, know there's only one sun.

So, there's no decision,
There's no choice but to suffer.
To lose my mind,
So, call me blind.

Call me Mad.
Call me Sad.
But deep down inside,
I'm frighteningly glad.

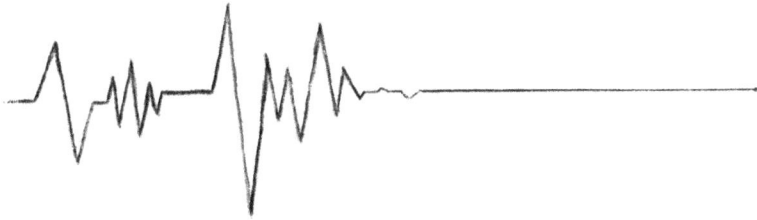

Broken Wings.

My lover brought me rest,
While I shook her tree.

No wonder she crashed,
Birds with broken wings do that.

If only I had been water and not fire.
If only I could have been the healer;

And not the healed.

Black Knight.

Society took a virgin,
A black-haired beauty.
Convinced this maiden,
It was her duty.

She was the sacrifice,
Lamb to slaughter.
Collateral damage,
World's angelic daughter.

Locked away from life,
She was kept.
Prepared for fate,
While monster slept.

Led down in tears,
Chained to docks.
Was our living salvation,
A way out for sordid nation.

But I refused,
And on went scaled armour.
I burned with purpose,
And shook with clamour.

Was my hero's quest,
Glory or death.
I readied my sword,
And crept with stealth.

I left in darkness,
Toward her light.
My sharp heels dug in,
Ready for fight.

Every step an effort,
Winds pounding sore.
I slowly closed in,
Along fated black shore.

At touching point,
She screamed aloud.
I whirled about,
For monster was around.

But still I could not see,
Nor vile dragon lashed.
The coward was invisible,
So away I slashed.

But still nothing,
Not a single striking blow.
I whirled about,
And ducked down low.

The maiden still shrieked,
So I turned to her.
I moved in close,
To calm her fear.

But then I saw,
In her eyes so clear.
The reflection brutal,
Ink eyes so truthful.

There was no monster,
There was no villain,
Because I was the devourer,
The destructive dragon.

The shock, the silence,
The horror and rage.
I lashed out with claw,
And freed her cage.

And in her face,
Fear changed to anger.
She struck out with dagger,
For I was the real danger.

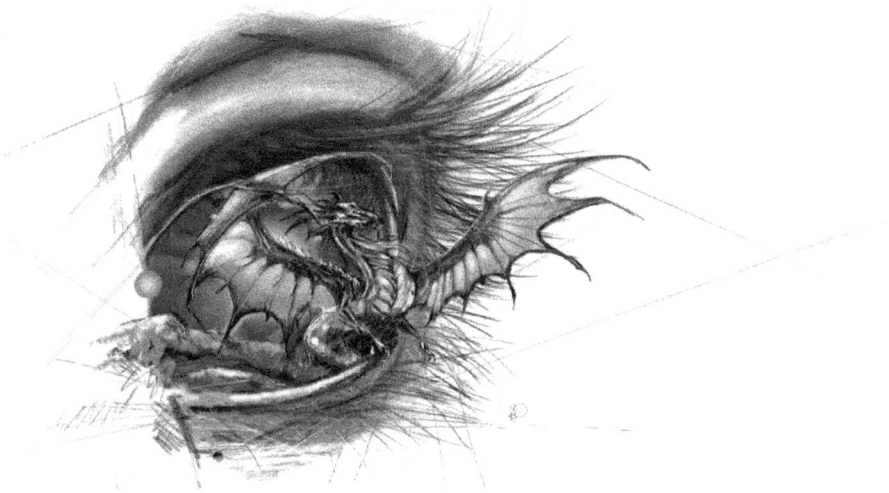

But bitterly,
The blow was not fatal.
I flew away,
Rejection terribly brutal.

Though dripping with blood,
It was the horror internal,
That destroyed my life,
Darkness infernal.

And on blackest of nights,
When the wind does howl,
There are no heroic knights,
Just bitter twisted dragon's growl.

This Dark Place.

There is a dark place,
That I can't go.

This dark place,
Comes to me.

It visits more often,
These days.

This dark place.

Wounds.

They just don't understand,
That this pain would be easier,
If I was
Bashed
Thrashed
Crashed
Mashed.

If only they knew,
That this is nothing,
Compared to
Fractured bones
Being stoned
Thrown from home
Lost alone.

I've been mugged,
By three thugs,
Cracked my ribs
Unconscious on drip
Near death twice
Suicidal vices.

But people don't see,
This is killing me.

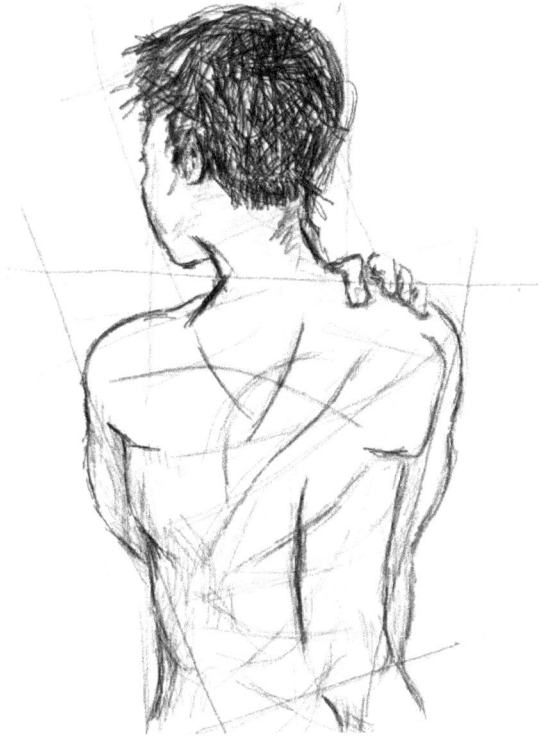

Give Me Numbness.

I'll take whatever you have,
Just to numb this pain.

To stop my chest aching,
To stop my will breaking.

Make me numb,
But not too numb.
I still have to function.

Caveman.

Why don't I just cave in,
And go back,
To being a caveman.

Oh.

Oh, that you had not loved me so much
Oh, that you would have had an ugly spirit
Oh, that I was repelled by dark, dark eyes
Then I would be an unconscious pain-free spirit

Oh, that you held me with physical force
Instead of the gentle soft manner that
Healed my soul and made me believe again
But you do that only to break me even worse

From purgatory and grey skies
You plucked me with gigantic butterfly wings
Holding me tight we soared in coloured skies
But I didn't realise that you were going to drop
me to hell

How unfortunate spirit am I to have been in Eden
And then cast out of Paradise
At least Adam was cast out with Eve
But you have left me alone with myself

Of course, your heart would tell other stories
Of how I manipulated, lied and ruined
Oh, if only we could meet beyond right and wrong
Do you understand what could be found?

No One.

It's not that you are a no one.
It's that you are a no one to someone.

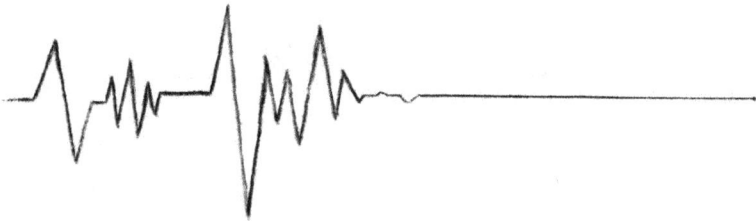

Break Through

Sometimes it takes an overwhelming breakdown to have an undeniable breakthrough.
Unknown.

Tears.

There are tears on this page...

But that's okay.

It's pain leaving my body.

Condemned.

The man faced the jury,
Broken, thin and without fury.
They stared at him with malice,
Their contempt was stirred and poisonous.

He could barely stand upright,
He grasped the railing and his plight.
There was an ice-cold air of tension,
The tiles were polished in anticipation.

The air was stayed and clinical,
The guards were present and physical.
The court was a whited sepulchre,
Justice hid like a trespasser.

The judges entered like executioners,
Their faces set like hungry vipers.
As they passed him in manner dim,
The accused wilted in exhaustion grim.

His crime was spelt out in fiery brimstone,
His accusers railed at him from iron throne.
Each word pieced him to the core,
Each stated claim rung his heart sore.

In his desperation he poured out his heart,
He admitted his failings and his tarnished part.
But on the matter of guilt he rejected theory,
He gave it all and told his truthful story.

And when he finished with all he said,
He visibly buckled and dropped his head.
No one stood for him or held him aloft
The tears that fell were audibly scoffed.

Nothing was said, the silence was screaming,
As he finally looked up, he felt the scheming.
The jury slowly stood, heavy and hard,
The accusers scowled, their faces marred.

And in the silence of a painted tomb,
The judges mocked his impending doom.
With satisfaction of hated right,
They crashed down his solitary life.

But with cowardice glee and unspoken word,
They wouldn't sentence or swing the sword.
The noose was never tied or hung,
The bullets were discarded from loaded gun.

Cruelty ruled his prisoned days,
Malice was served in agonised delay.
A one-sided story would hold sway,
History was corrupted in almighty play.

They'd keep him alive in rotting cell,
Awaking him each dawn from wretched hell.
And while he wasted away, barely alive,
Each moment his torturer stood grim and vile.

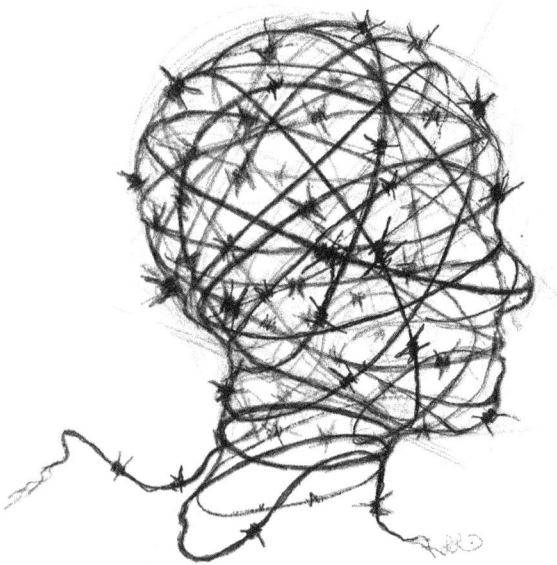

The freedom of love had turned to hate,
He was destined to live in cutting fate.
What once was his life's breathing blood,
Robbed him of peace in mind's ungodly flood.

His punishment didn't befit his crimes,
Perhaps his guilt came from not reading signs.
He became the man firmly in the iron mask,
A mind clouded, robbed and beaten in task.

And despite the constant agony and wounds,
He couldn't die or escape living doom.
He wasn't able to find more tears to cry,
He desired peace but was kept alive by Why.

He began to beg daily for peaceful release,
A cup of poison to allow torture to cease.
But nothing brought him any beautiful peace,
And the demons inside and out continued to feast.

But then in quiet, dark solitary night,
A soft white dove visited him in small delight.
The little creature sat with him in calm respite,
She brought a small seed to help his plight.

And at that moment the tiny, single seed,
Began to grow and his soul to feed.
The message came and, in his mind, did show,
He was his own torturer and he could let go.

And despite the injustice and grievous acclaim,
The prisoner let go and forgave his blame.
In the quiet, restless wicked night,
He let go and let himself die.

Happiness on the Inside.

Alone at a table,
Rarely feeling stable.
Seeking answers and revelation,
Trying desperately for elevation.

There was a man around,
But now he's gone and I'm drowned,
With anxiety, emptiness and depression,
I've dropped into hopeless recession.

I grimace at my current prison,
I know by now I should have risen.
From the edge of this terror and despair,
On to tomorrow and all of its care.

But something holds me back,
I'm stunned and begin to retract.
Bony icy fingers being to enclose,
Causing more awful, woeful throes.

And as the sun slowly sets,
Along comes the past and its regrets.
A slow bruising ancient caravan,
Rolling continuously with no forward plan.

Head feels like I'm a wounded soldier,
I can't stop being this cannon fodder.
A war rages through with total aplomb,
I only sink further like a dying swan.

Truth be told I couldn't feel worse,
In vain do I try to correct this verse?
The quagmire is still rising slowly,
Sucking me away in a state so lowly.

But through the plaguing of my soul,
A single thought comes and bores a hole.
Where is the glimmer of hope?
How can I end this sliding slope?

The herd of wild thoughts rush on by,
I let them go and begin to know why.
They belong elsewhere in another place,
Somehow, I'm going to get through this phase.

And slowly light does brighten grass green,
I let those terrible thoughts go and be mean.
And within a small light smile I confide,
We can be free and happy on the inside.

Stop!

(These thoughts again...)

I'm Dead.
I'm shattered.
I'm broken.
It's over.
It's the end.

This is my end.

STOP!

You're just in pain.
And it will pass.

Now what will you turn this suffering into?

Hey Dude!

Hey Dude.
Fix the attitude.
It's okay to be in solitude.
But you need to add gratitude.

Gratitude + Solitude = The Best Attitude.

Smart about Love.

There's nothing smart about love
It's a stupid emotion
That requires ultimate devotion
To a whirlwind of desires
And stokes the fires
Flames
The hurricanes
Sounds like a fucking nightmare
A scene of carnage
Like Godzilla's rage
Like a desperate man in a cage

I'm tellin' ya there's nothing smart about love

Ask Romeo how it worked out
Juliet turned out like a class decision
Stupidity turned to precision
They should've added a dose of pessimism
But no, they decided on a conclusion
Reducing their chance of intellectual survival
Through lust revival
They blundered around like a carnival
Before a maddening finale
Driven bananas
Damn, what animals

There's nothing smart about love

Green-eyed vixen sits in the corner
Sipping on a cocktail
Throw two parts of insanity
One part humanity
Four parts profanity
Then you have a cocktail ready to drink
Grind the pour fool into the sink
And the vixen to boot
Soon he's in a suit
Walking down the aisle
Before choking down bile

I tell you there's nothing smart about love

Fools rush in where angels play golf

Blindly we flail

Missing the howl of the wolf

Wretched humans and our impending doom

There's always room

To expand the gloom

Let go of control

Become full throttle

Double down infatuation

Hype up heart's inflation

Star crossed in damnation

I tell you there's nothing smart about love

Boom he said
He should have had his head read
Solomon said better to be dead
But he said boom!
Cause he walked in the door
Pretty girl
Damn amazing curl
Which had to unfurl
At such times
That built rhymes
In his heart and stole his smarts
Like a gibbering idiot
He had to fidget and said boom!

I tell you there's nothing smart about love

She hated the fact
That she always had to act
He never returned the calls
And stupidly she had to fall
In the first place
A race to the bottom of the IQ pit
Falling was a familiar calling
Resulting in all his bawling
The loneliness and pain
When there was nothing left to gain
Just all the shame
Of falling so hard and fast
Not learning from the past

I tell you there's nothing smart about love

But what choice do we really have
How can we really behave?
Clinically, finickity, another city
Hell no, because we all like stupidity
For a chance for serendipity
To feel ourselves falling again
To find a way to mend
Yes, you might be going around the bend
But there's magic to be had
Fire to warm
Let the heart swarm
With all these stupid thoughts

I tell you there's nothing like falling in love

Feel the Fire.

It's better to feel the burn,
Rather than to learn.

For it's better felt than telt.

The End.

The

      End,

           Is

                Not

                    The

                        End;

                    The

                End,

            Is

        The

Mend.

Hope.

Hope begins with a pinprick of light
A single dot of reasonable delight
It starts with a solitary feeling
A burst of joy to face the grieving

A moment in time to accept joy
A split second of energy to face the toil
A zephyr of ecstasy to feel in heart
A microcosm to begin and start

A single pebble against unholy floods
A tiny effort against the seeping blood
A small twitch to shake the devastation
A minute uprising against wicked nation

Four small letters against crooked alphabet
A smallish risk with a mighty heft
Against the hopeless despair
A small seed to plant and begin repair

A single ant crawls out of dark hole
His advance against earth with spirited soul
A child is born helpless and weak
Transforms cries of pain in strengthened feat

The little bud appears on dried branch
A single spark emerges out of broken trance
From the darkness comes speck of light
Promising vigour and renewed fight

From nothing comes a little something
From emptiness comes something to cling
A solitary dog in vast wilderness
A slight touch in gentle tenderness

Sleep is woken with single beat
Coldness is attacked with whitish heat
This beautiful hope though small in size
Has started an avalanche of giant rise.

Change.

Sometimes life can be so furious
Trapped in a cycle so superfluous
Not knowing why
Not knowing how
Not knowing where
It's hard to care

This pattern won't stop repeating
It's hard to live a life so self-defeating
You want to make change
You want to stop rage
You want to find the way
To climb out of this cage

Days roll by with excruciating pain
The wind never stops, nor does the rain
There must be a plan
To find a new man
There must be a life
Away from all this strife

On top a mountain never stop musing
There's time to cry and time for amusing
Thoughts are like bugs
Eating away with the buzz
The mind never ends
The soul never mends

But then a lightbulb moment
Clarity without resentment
I can make this change
I can break out of these chains
This pattern can finish
And the dullness diminish

It's happening right now, this almighty desire
It's happening to me like a cleansing fire
I can end this God-awful pattern
I can become someone who's pure platinum
I will make this stand
This I will demand

Now it's happened to me
And I've broken away free
The old man is dead
I do not fear to tread
This new life is great
I'm alive, not succumbed to fate.

Get.

If you don't get her,
You don't get her.

If they didn't get you,
They didn't get you.

Get her and you will get her.
Get them and they will get you.

When it Rains, it Pours!

When it rains, it pours
And your pores seem flawed
Even the floors aren't straight
The straits are rocking and crashing
And rocks become boulders
And you're constantly bowled over.

The hills seem like mountains
You feel like you're mounted to the spot
Spotting the future but rooted to the past
And your time feels like it has passed you
You've mistimed your jump
And the hump cannot be jumped.

The smallest pain feels like a roaring wound
And you've wound up at a stop sign
Assigned the loser's tag
While been tagged with a laden bag
That cannot be unbagged
You've been left to carry the can.

The current is going the other way
And currently you feel like you hold no sway
Beholden to drag every step
The steppes seem higher every day
And your hire button never gets pushed
While your enemies are holding a Putsch.
Each blow rains in harder

The reigns are slipping from your hands
And even the handyman doesn't respond
Your body isn't responsive
Your body of work isn't impressive
And your life's story hasn't made the press.

And before you note it, you're demoted
The moat has increasingly grown wider
While you're none the wiser
And the nun is angrier
With self-righteous anger
And ready to administer the last rites.

And despite all your foes
And all of your faux paus
You remember what Pa said
"All storm clouds must pass"
So, you storm on again
Through the rain, on to great gain.

Will.

What will be;
Will be.

What you will for;
Will be.

What you are willing for;
Will be.

Like Mum.

All my life,
I looked for someone like Mum.

I just didn't realise,
I had to be someone like Dad.

Understand.

Sometimes it's understand;
and go.

Sometimes it's just stand;
and go.

Do the Thing.

Do the thing that gives you peace,
Not puts you in pieces.

There is a higher love.

Just One.

Just one letter,
Can start the healing process,
Just one word,
Can begin every triumphant success.

Just one look,
Can mend a broken heart,
Just one touch,
Can begin love's passionate start.

Just one hug,
Can help a grieving friend,
Just one kiss,
Can cause pain to start to end.

Just one moment,
Can give strength to another,
Just one smile,
Can help a lonely stranger.

Just one prayer,
Can turn a hard heart soft,
Just one thought,
Can make the mind soar aloft.

Just one day,
Can kick-start the rest of your life.
Just one hour,
Can turn away the internal strife.

Just one page,
Can reveal amazing power,
Just one story,
Can lift rubble into great big tower.

Just one chance,
To seize life from the shelf,
Just one minute,
To choose to be your true self.

Give Yourself to Joy.

Give yourself to Joy
In your Head
In your Heart
In your Mind

Give yourself to Joy
Find your way through Doubts
Through Fears
Through Anger

Give yourself to Joy
Take the time to let go of The Wrong
The Bad
The Unhelpful

Give yourself to Joy
Rest your Soul and be Present
Be Still
Be Quiet

Give yourself to Joy
Release the Anchors of the Past
Of the Future
Of the Unknown

Give yourself to Joy
Now's your Time to Hear the Music
To Feel the Love
To See the Beauty

Give Yourself to Joy

The Train of Grief.

You cannot fight this train,
You cannot run,
You cannot jump.

Lie Down and
Let the Train
Run Over you.

Lie down and be still;
And eventually it will pass.

Breakthrough.

The breakthrough

Comes when there is

Nothing

Left to break through.

Find a Way.

When it's difficult to breathe
And you're troubled and can't sleep
Don't consign yourself a fate
Don't clean off the slate

When the earth is opening up beneath
And life feels a distance reach
Don't give up and weep
Don't long for an eternal sleep

When birds stop humming and singing
And depression is in your ears ringing
Don't start hating and grieving
Don't fight and begin seething

You're not far from happiness
Soon you're in joy awareness
Stand up, jump, shout and say
I have the strength to find a way

When the doubters and critics roar
When you can't get up and soar
Don't throw in the towel
Don't get miffed and feel foul

When the air is stiff and polluted
When you've resigned or been booted
Now's not the time to give up
The bell's yet to ring and quit

When you shout, scream and weep
When the harvest does not reap
Don't stray from your commitment
Don't give in to negative sentiment

Sometimes our lives fall from grace
And we're running last in the race
Our desire wanes and drips
Our heart is torn and rips

Our moments and fear and doubt
Cleave us in two and rout
We fall over and wane
Our spirits disappear and strain

But inside is the ultimate winner
Not a doomed person or sinner
We are all beautiful creatures
With a future bright as beaches

Say it,
We'll find a way
Sing it,
We'll find a way
Shout it,
We'll find a way

A way, because there's always a way

Love.

Your job is not to destroy
The love in your heart.

Your job is making room,
And keeping the love there.

Love is never to be destroyed.
Good shouldn't be replaced with evil.

Suffering for Her.

Numbness. Breathless.
Senseless. Defenseless.

On this long vigil,
I'm getting restless.

Agitation. Stagnation.
Fascination. Transformation.

On my knees,
I'm waiting for emancipation.

Weeping. Energy depleting.
Heart's steeping. Eyes bleeding.

Tearfully, mournfully,
Agonies are heaping.

Emotions. Mind's commotion.
Faded motions. Ill notions.

Meditating,
She has my total devotion.

Once in a lifetime.
Your soul begins to chime.

She's worth suffering for.

On the Move.

Being on the move,
Is not moving on.

So for the first time,
I'll stop the climb.

And be still.

Ray of Sunlight.

Three days of hell over Easter.
Listening, listening but there was no speaker.

Sweat soaked sheets, matted hair,
Vacant eyes and a burning stare.

Losing weight, barely able to eat,
Time's agony while trying to sleep.

Sound cancelling headset on repeat,
Arms slumped in utter defeat.

Mumbling to oneself in anger,
Mind's migraine never-ending clangor.

Second night with a shocking fright,
The accuser came with fated height.

"Liar!" she screamed, pointed finger.
Horror stare, she stayed to linger.

"Manipulator!" she shrieked viciously.
 Closer she stalked with wicked intensity.

"Ruiner and Destroyer!" she shouted.
 By now my mind was utterly routed.

And with sweat and tears on my face,
I finally had the courage to face this fate.

I stood toe to toe with this thin spectre,
Instead of fighting I became a respecter.

I reached out and let this hating ghost,
Enter my body, I became the host.

And for a while my knees twisted and buckled,
I held onto the ground shaking, white knuckled.

Then the mind was broken and body dead,
All that was left was the spirit that bled.

And the lightness lifted like a white dove,
Because I realised I was bleeding pure love.

And like a reborn soul I stood tall,
I gave myself to utter love, big and small.

I closed my eyes and saw the beautiful spirit,
Whispering "I Love You"; I became fearless.

And as miracles should be, I began to see,
Something that would forever make me free.

Through the window, through cloud and haze,
Out shone a blinding light, a single Ray.

Crossroads.

A man stood at the crossroads,
Looking about.
He contemplated life,
And wondered out loud.

Through pain and tempest,
The emotions blew hot.
He cracked his knuckles,
He couldn't stay in this spot.

Frost talked about the hard way,
The road less travelled.
He agonised over decisions,
He wondered which he favoured.

The stable side with perks,
With appearance and worth.
Or the dreamer's path,
Where dangers may lurk.

On one hand a structure,
The other pure nature.
One choice a label,
The other with flavour.

Which had more good
And less evil?
Which would provide comfort?
It was dicing with the devil.

He sighed in his outlook,
And knew what to do.
Risks were worth taking,
It was the lot of a few.

Not all things worked out,
Fairy-tales were free.
Society's fables,
Leads the masses to be.

With determine he smiled,
And left the shadows.
He rode out on luck,
Opposite pale meadows.

The twinkling of lights,
The darkness of path,
The danger above,
But he followed his heart.

A Higher Love.

It is the Everest,
This Higher Love.

It is the Platinum of Platinums,
This Higher Love.

It is greater than life,
This Higher Love.

It's above the greatest orgasm,
This Higher Love.

It is the antidote to all suffering,
This Higher Love.

It is better than the closest of closeness,
This Higher Love.

Let go of everything until you have;
This Higher Love.

Conclusion.

Better, not bitter. Mend, not end.
Learn, not burn. Sweet, not sweat.
Up, not uppers. Reset, not resent.

Love, not hate.

Always and Ever.

A Big Thank You.

For those of you who have bothered to purchase this book and read it, I thank you kindly.

For those of you who have understood the madness of a creative spirit and been supportive; I thank you from the bottom of the heart.

To the contributors to the book and those from the Godsforge team, thank you. I look forward to the next book about to hit production.

Finally, to the beautiful spirit out there, words cannot express the thankfulness for receiving the gift of unconditional love.

Leanne Larson

Leanne is an Award-winning artist born and raised in Rural NSW, Australia and currently residing in Central Minnesota, USA.

Leanne has a strong desire to connect, inspire, and empower others through her art. Much of her work are illustrations and paintings that portray narrative vignettes of her past. The content is cathartic, and the subject matter illustrates the human condition.

She also loves to share her creative space with others by physically painting 'live' on-site at events including, weddings fundraisers corporate events and more.

Leanne has her work in both private and public collections throughout the USA and Australia. Including the permanent collection in the Briggs Library at the University of Minnesota. In 2011 & 2012 she won the Lois P. Hodgell printmaking award.

Rachel Sadler

Rachel is a writer, editor and all-round creative soul.

Her intense love for words led to a degree in journalism and literature, followed by a spanning career in advertising — helping brands to fine-tune their written communications.

However, she had a burning desire to use her talents for good, thus created her own writing and editing label, righting house.

Through righting house, Rachel pursues purposeful work – whether it's co-authoring self-help books, editing impactful autobiographies or blogging about real-world issues.

As an emotionally-charged right-brainer, she believes in the power of words. It's her goal to collaborate on books that serve a greater purpose.

About Godsforge

Godsforge is a creative agency and publishing business dedicated to artists all over the globe. Publishing your work in a very competitive and complex world is difficult, so Godsforge works hard to bring art to the eye of the public. Our motto is:

"We're better by creating together."

You can find out more by visiting www.godsforge.com

20 percent of all profits goes to The 360 Foundation which is dedicated to empowering individuals through technology, training and education in the Developing World.

You can read more about our foundation by visiting – www.the360foundation.com

αγάπη

www.ingramcontent.com/pod-product-compliance
Lightning Source LLC
LaVergne TN
LVHW041153080426
835511LV00006B/582